# Waiting for Messiah

# Waiting for Messiah

Remembering Easter 2020

Rainbow Chang

RESOURCE *Publications* • Eugene, Oregon

WAITING FOR MESSIAH
Remembering Easter 2020

Copyright © 2021 Rainbow Chang. All rights reserved. Except for brief quotations in critical publications or reviews, no part of this book may be reproduced in any manner without prior written permission from the publisher. Write: Permissions, Wipf and Stock Publishers, 199 W. 8th Ave., Suite 3, Eugene, OR 97401.

Resource Publications
An Imprint of Wipf and Stock Publishers
199 W. 8th Ave., Suite 3
Eugene, OR 97401

www.wipfandstock.com

PAPERBACK ISBN: 978-1-7252-9067-9
HARDCOVER ISBN: 978-1-7252-9068-6
EBOOK ISBN: 978-1-7252-9069-3

02/01/21

It is written as a play. It provides actions like life painting performance and life music performance on the stage, and also religious ritual like Pascal Seder, Holy Communion, micro observation with magnifying glasses of insects, Coronavirus and space exploration with telescope and live event of launching rocket to the space by SpaceX in Florida Kennedy Space Centre.

The pictures in this book were the drawings produced by my daughter Arabella during the Easter season 2020. At the time, she has just turned 4 years old. These wonderful drawings, I hope, are not only part of the remembering of Easter 2020 for me and for her personally, and also represents the beautiful resilience of our shared humanity towards suffering, death and fear. we might have faced the darkest hour, we are facing the darkest hour and we will face the darkest hour but we shall rise. We shall rise and upheld with the beautiful things in our hands which we have created in the darkest hours, and we shall rise up and uphold beauty within us as God will raise us up more than we can be.

Rainbow Chang, Oxford, July 2020

**Starting Time:** 7:30pm on the 8th of April 2020 First night of Passover Seder, remembering the night of Passover in Egypt 1300 BC and the night of Last Supper of Lord Jesus Christ with his disciples in AD 33.

**Place:** Arabella in her back garden with mummy during the lock down of the 2020 pandemic at their home in the city centre of Oxford, by the Thames River.

**Characters:** Arabella, Mummy and the snail. Arabella is a 4 years old girl. Mummy is a religious Christian writer and a single mother.

**Scene:** There is a big and old cherry tree on the north corner of the garden. The branches of the cherry tree cover 60 percent of the garden. The white cherry flowers are in full blossom during the Easter season.

# Passover Seder/ The Last Supper, 8th of April 2020

*Arabella is sitting on her swing.*

**Arabella:**
There is so much to do in our garden, mummy.
I have swing, sea-saw, trampoline, slides, play house, art studio, hula hoops, skip rope, tennis rockets, balls, magnifying glasses, telescope, bird feeder.

*Mummy sitting under the green umbrella under the cherry tree and playing a harp with a shofar and a Bible on the table.*

**Mummy:** "Yes, Arabella, we are very lucky."

**Mummy:** "The sun is going down soon, shall we have Seder in the garden."

**Arabella:** "I wish we could go to Levi's house for Passover."

**Mummy:** "Well, we can go to the planet Mars for Passover next year, but, we are in our garden now, hooray, lets enjoy ourselves, shall we? I will play you psalm 136 to start with."

*Harp music played by Mummy and sing Psalm 136.*

# Waiting for Messiah

Give thanks to the Lord, for he is good.
His love endures forever.
Give thanks to the God of gods
His love endures forever.
Give thanks to the Lord of lords:
His love endures forever.
to him who alone does great wonders,
His love endures forever.
who by his understanding made the heavens,
His love endures forever.
who spread out the earth upon the waters,
His love endures forever.
who made the great lights—
His love endures forever.
the sun to govern the day,
His love endures forever.
the moon and stars to govern the night;
His love endures forever.
to him who struck down the firstborn of Egypt
His love endures forever.
and brought Israel out from among them
His love endures forever.
with a mighty hand and outstretched arm;
His love endures forever.
to him who divided the Red Sea
asunder
His love endures forever.
and brought Israel through the midst of it,
His love endures forever.
but swept Pharaoh and his army into the Red Sea;
His love endures forever.
to him who led his people through the wilderness;
His love endures forever.
to him who struck down great kings,
His love endures forever.
 and killed mighty kings—
His love endures forever.

*Passover Seder/ The Last Supper, 8th of April 2020*

Sihon king of the Amorites
His love endures forever.
and O king of Bashan—
His love endures forever.
and gave their land as an inheritance,
His love endures forever.
an inheritance to his servant Israel.
His love endures forever.
He remembered us in our low estate
His love endures forever.
and freed us from our enemies.
His love endures forever.

He gives food to every creature.
His love endures forever.
Give thanks to the God of heaven.
His love endures forever.
(the end of Psalm 136)

**Arabella:**
Blossoming cherry tree in our garden
Pure white
From branch to branch
Thames river passing by
Pure water
From distance to distance
Mummy:
The plague is covering the earth
Pure darkness
From land to land
Arabella and I are getting ready for Pascal
The shared matzo
Pure bread
From Egypt to Jerusalem
The body of Jesus
From heaven to earth
Arabella:

The sun we could not see is setting
Pure light
From somewhere to somewhere
The passing over is tonight

**Mummy:**
1300BC, tonight
Israel sat down in lock down in Egypt for a hurried meal and ready to travel
From slavery to freedom
**Arabella:**
33AD, tonight
Jesus sat down for the last time in Jerusalem for his last supper and ready to travel from the valley of death and hell to free mankind
**Mummy:**
2020AD, tonight
Millions people are dying from hunger tonight
The old and the young
Millions people are suffering from hunger
The old and the young
Even when the Israelis lived as slaves in ancient Egypt they had plenty food to eat
What are you feeling tonight
What are you doing tonight
**Arabella:**
2020AD, tonight
Children are working as slaves tonight
Women are trafficked as slaves tonight
Millions are slaves and barely survive tonight
The Israelites cry for justice was heard by their God
Their God delivered them from slavery tonight
Who can hear me tonight
Can you hear your own cry for freedom tonight
**Mummy:**
Once again, the Israeli nation is in lock down from plague tonight
This time not in Egypt but in the land of their own
No one died from the plague in Egypt

### Passover Seder/ The Last Supper, 8th of April 2020

But many died in the promised land
How to celebrate Passover Seder tonight
What are the questions our children shall ask
The wise
The wicked
The simple
And the one does Not know how to question
Where to search for the question
Where to search for the answer
**Arabella:**
2020AD, tonight
We celebrate this Passover Seder
The past, the present, the future and the beyond time all at the table of tonight
I am hungry
I want to be free

*(Silence)*

*Mummy is blowing the shofar. The sound of shofar breaks the silence.*

**Arabella:**
Mummy, I am hungry now, can we have dinner please?
**Mummy:**
Yes, hurry
It is the time now
The sun is setting down
Tonight is the Passover Seder
Tonight is the last supper of Jesus Christ
**Arabella:**
What is this meal about?
**Mummy:**
It is about our earthly life
It is our story as history and poetry
**Arabella:**
Is our earthly life important to God
So that He tells us what to eat and how to eat?

**Mummy:**
Our earthly life is important to God
He provides enough food for all to eat
And He tells us what to eat and how to eat
**Arabella:**
God provides enough food for all to eat?
But there are millions lives are dying of hunger tonight
**Mummy:**
Yes, millions lives are dying of hunger tonight
Because we have stolen their bread
**Arabella:**
Shall we eat tonight?
The bread with innocent blood
While many souls are dying of hunger?
**Mummy:**
We shall eat
We shall eat
The bread of life tonight
For you
For me
For all the hungry souls tonight
**Arabella:**
Should we eat our sister and brother's bread while they are dying from hunger?
**Mummy:**
We shall eat
We shall eat this bread of life with our brothers and sisters together tonight
Like the last supper of Christ
May this bread transform suffering to joy
May this bread give life beyond bread
**Arabella:**
Many are dying of hunger
Food
Many are living in slavery
Freedom
Many are dying of this plague

## Passover Seder/ The Last Supper, 8th of April 2020

Air
What shall we do with this bread in our hands
This bread for hunger
This bread for eternal life
In lock down
In a small town
**Mummy:**
Many are dying of hunger
Food
Many are dying of slavery
Freedom
Many are dying of the plague
Breath
What shall we do with this bread in our hands
This bread for hunger
This bread for eternal life
In lock down
In a small town
Let's share it
Let's share it in our mind
Let's share it with our brothers and sisters in our minds
**Mummy:**
Let's Share it
Share the bread for hunger
Food for all
Let's share it
Share the bread for eternal life
Freedom for all
Let's share it
Share the air of air
Breath of life for all
In our garden,
At our home
With the imagination of our minds
We share the bread with all people

From me to you

From you to me
It goes around around and around
We pretend it goes around the world
Around, around and around
**Arabella:**
Let's share it
Share the bread for hunger
Food for all
Let's share it
Share the bread for eternal life
Freedom for all
Let's share it
Share the air of air
Breath for life for all
In our garden
At our home
With the imagination of our hearts
We share the bread with all people
From me to you
From you to me
It goes around, around and around
We pretend it goes around the world
Around, around and around
**Mummy:**
Hurry up
It is the time
**Arabella:**
Don't forget give some bread to the snail.
**Mummy:**
Of course, the snail.

*They break the matzo, passing on to each other and eat. Arabella gives some bread to the snail.*

**Arabella:**
Let's imagine that we are leaving the land of Egypt now and standing in front of the Red Sea

## Passover Seder/ The Last Supper, 8th of April 2020

Who shall walk into the water first?
You or me?
**Mummy:**
Let's imagine that we are leaving the land of Egypt now and standing in front of the Red Sea
Who shall walk into the water first?
You or me?
Me, of course, because you will be sitting on my shoulder
**Arabella:**
Let's imagine that we are leaving the land of Egypt now and standing in front of the Red Sea
who shall walk into the water first?
you or me?
We shall walk into the water together
My small hand in your big hand
**Mummy:**
Let's imagine that we are leaving the land of Egypt now and standing in front of the Red Sea
Who shall walk into the water first?
You or me?
We shall walk into the water together
My big hand in your small hand
**Arabella:**
Let's imagine we meet God face to face
Who will embrace him first
You or me?
**Mummy:**
Let's imagine we meet God face to face
Who will embrace him first
You or me?
You, of course, because you are the innocent

**Arabella:**
Let's imagine we meet God face to face
Who will embrace him first
You or me?
I am the child in your tummy
We embrace God together of course.
**Mummy:**
Yes, of course, you and me are one together
Embrace the one who made us all.
Arabella: One free is not free
We shall all be free tonight
When I am free
You are free with me

*They seesaw together in the garden.*

**Arabella:**
Why is this night different from other nights?
**Mummy:**
Because of you
Why is this night different from other nights?
**Arabella:**
Because of me
Why is this night different from other nights?
**Mummy:**
Because of those people fighting with the Coronavirus
Why is this night different from other nights?
**Arabella:**
Because of those hungry mouths and hungry souls dying for bread
Why is this night different from other nights?
**Mummy:**
Because tonight we remember the night man was freed by divine and divine was locked by man
Why is this night different from other nights?
**Arabella:**
Because tonight is tonight
Why is this night different from other nights?

### Passover Seder/The Last Supper, 8th of April 2020

**Mummy:**
Because tonight is tonight
The Israelites called Joseph 'Joseph'
And the bone of Joseph rose up from the river Nile
**Arabella:**
Because tonight is tonight
Why is this night different from other nights
**Mummy:**
Because tonight is tonight
You and me, together, under the blossoming cherry tree
At home
In Oxford
A small town
You and me
Remember
The tree
You and me
Tonight

# Good Friday, 10th of April 2020

*Under the blossoming cherry tree*
*Arabella uses magnify glasses to observe the snails and insects.*
*A big screen shows the Coronavirus under microscope being studied by scientists in Oxford.*

**Arabella:**
Mummy, the snail is sick, he might have got the Coronavirus.
**Mummy:**
How do you know?
**Arabella:**
He is not moving
**Mummy:**
He might be just meditating
Don't disturb him

*Arabella bouncing on trampoline*
*Mummy is on her iPad*

**Arabella:**
Mummy, I am hungry
**Mummy:**
I said that we won't eat today
It's Good Friday
Jesus suffered and died on the Cross for us

## Good Friday, 10th of April 2020

We remember that
**Arabella:**
Did Jesus die on the Cross for the snail too?
Can the snail eat today?
**Mummy:**
Ask the snail

**Arabella:**
Snail,
It's Good Friday today
We remember Jesus suffered and died for us on the Cross
I am not eating today
Are you going to eat or not?
**Snail:**
Silence
**Arabella:**
Why are you not talking?
**Snail:**
Silence
**Arabella:**
Mummy, the snail is not talking
**Mummy:**
He did talk. He said silence.
**Arabella:**
No, he didn't. I did not hear that.
**Mummy:**
Well, I did.

**Arabella:**
Mummy, did Jesus die for the snail too
**Mummy:**
Ask the snail
**Arabella:**
I told you the snail is not talking
**Mummy:**
Oh, ask Jesus then

**Arabella:**
You said that He is dying on the Cross today, how can I ask Him when he is dying
**Mummy:**
Ask him on Easter Sunday then
**Arabella:**
I can't wait for Easter Sunday
**Mummy:**
You can wait for the chocolate Easter eggs
**Arabella:**
Yes, yes, I can't wait to eat the chocolate Easter eggs

**Mummy:**
Shall we paint Jesus on the Cross?
**Arabella:**
Yeah, I love to paint.

*Mummy brought out easel, canvas, paints and brushes*

*Arabella draws and paints*

**Arabella:**
Why did Jesus die on the Cross for us?
**Mummy:**
Why did Jesus die on the Cross for us?
**Arabella:**
Why are you not answering my question?
**Mummy:**
Why are you not answering my question?
**Arabella:**
You are the mummy, I am not the mummy.
**Mummy:**
Why does mummy have to answer questions?
**Arabella:**
Stop talking, be quiet
**Mummy:**
Why

## Good Friday, 10th of April 2020

**Arabella:**
I am not going to tell you, it's a secret

*Arabella paints Jesus on the Cross, Mummy helps.*

**Arabella:**
I am hungry, mummy
**Mummy:**
It's lucky that you are feeling hungry.
Many people died today from the Coronavirus
They don't feel hungry any more.
**Arabella:**
You said Jesus also died today
**Mummy:**
Yes, Jesus died 2000 years ago today
Many people have died today
All died today, but a different today
**Arabella:**
Are we going to remember all of those people who died today like we remember Jesus?
**Mummy:**
Yes, we shall remember them.
hey all shall be remembered
**Arabella:**
Like Jesus
**Mummy:**
The death of Jesus is different
**Arabella:**
Why is the death of Jesus different
**Mummy:**
Because Jesus is the Messiah
through his death, death shall be no more one day
**Arabella:**
You just said that many people have died today because of the Coronavirus.

**Mummy:**
Yes, many people have also died because of hunger, many people have died today for different reasons.
But death shall be no more one day.
**Arabella:**
When is one day mummy?
**Mummy:**
One day is the day I do not know
One day is the day you do not know
One day is the day we all know
One day is one day
One day is the day
One day could be today
Do you like my little poem Arabella?
**Arabella:**
You like the rhyming rabbit.
**Mummy:**
Hehehe, you mean the one from Julia Donaldson's story?
**Arabella:**
Yes.

*Arabella paints Jesus on the Cross, mummy helps.*

**Arabella:**
Are you going to die mummy?
**Mummy:**
Yes, we all are going to die one day
When I am dead, you shall put me in a treasure box
When you die, your children will put you in a treasure box
And lay yours next to mine
Jesus loves treasure hunts
He will find us in treasure boxes
We are his treasures
**Arabella:**
I want a heart shape treasure box to hide when I am dead

## Good Friday, 10th of April 2020

**Mummy:**
Good idea
Can you paint my treasures box rainbow colour please?
**Arabella:**
Are the people died from the Coronavirus all in treasure boxes and wait for Jesus find them
**Mummy:**
Yes, for sure, many treasure boxes laid down to hid for the treasure hunt today.

*Arabella paints Jesus on the Cross, mummy helps.*
**Arabella:**
Can Jesus still find me if I hide in my treasure box on Mars after I die?
**Mummy:**
You want to die on Mars?
**Arabella:**
You said that if I go to Mars in a space rocket, I might not come back
**Mummy:**
I meant you might die between the earth and the Mars
**Arabella:**
Where is that?
**Mummy:**
Space
**Arabella:**
I will hide in my treasure box after I die next to yours in space?
**Mummy:**
Well, you might not be exactly next to me, because everything floating around in space
**Arabella:**
Like the flying carpet
**Mummy:**
Yes, exactly, like the flying carpet
**Arabella:**
Why are we all going to die mummy?

**Mummy:**
Why are we all going to die Arabella?
**Arabella:**
Why don't you answer my question?
**Mummy:**
Why don't you answer my question?
**Arabella:**
Shh, be quite, I think the snail is talking
**Mummy:**
What is the snail talking about?
**Arabella:**
It's secret, I am not going to tell you
**Mummy:**
Well, the snail's brain has been stored on the computer, so I shall google it.
What he thinks and talks won't be secret to me anymore.
**Arabella:**
The internet is very slow like the snail
It will be just loading and loading, and loading. . . . .

*Mummy and Arabella laugh together and paint on each other.*

# Easter Sunday, 12th of April 2020

*Craft Easter eggs and Markers pens are on the table under the cherry tree.*
*Arabella and Mummy are painting the craft eggs with Markers pens. There are also chocolate Easter eggs wrapped in many colours in a basket.*

**Arabella:**
Robin! Robin! Mummy, look, Robin is here!
**Mummy:**
Shh, be quite, leave the poor Robin alone
He doesn't want to be disturbed.
**Arabella:**
Mummy, Robin is eating a caterpillar!
**Mummy:**
That's ok.
The caterpillar will be free in the sky like the Tibetans being freed by vultures after they are dead.
**Arabella:**
I want to be free in the sky
**Mummy:**
Yes you will, but not with robins or vultures, you are going to be free on earth and in the sky with Jesus after the resurrection.
**Arabella:**
When Mummy? I want to be flying in the sky now!

**Mummy:**
Well, today is Easter Sunday
How about you wear your angel costume with the big wings and fly around?
**Arabella:**
Yes, yes, I want to wear my angel costume with wings.

*Mummy takes out Arabella's angel costume and helps her to put it on. Arabella flies around the garden with her wings.*

**Mummy:**
Arabella, how about we play the resurrection scene from the Bible? I play Marry Magdalene and you play the angel and we pretend this basket of chocolate eggs is the resurrected Jesus.
**Arabella:**
I love to play angel! Let's play, let's play?

*They play the scene when Mary met the resurrected Jesus outside of the tomb in John 20:1*

**Mummy:**
Now, it's the time to eat the chocolate eggs.
**Arabella:**
Hooray, I love chocolate eggs.
**Mummy:**
Many people are dead and dying today in the world right now because of the virus,
Let's remember them in a minute of silence before we eat, shall we?
**Arabella:**
Yes mummy.

*They bow their head for one minute in remembering the people died from the virus and the dying in the four corners of the world.*

## Easter Sunday, 12th of April 2020

**Arabella:**
Why was Jesus resurrected on Easter Sunday?

**Mummy:**
So that no more death from life can bring sorrow and no more separation from God can bring suffering.

**Arabella:**
Are we going to be resurrected after we die?

**Mummy:**
Yes, but not right away. We have to wait for Jesus come back to earth again and find us in our treasure boxes.

**Arabella:**
Can Jesus find the caterpillar that has been eaten by the robin and resurrect him? The caterpillar did not hide himself in a treasure box, because he was eaten by the robin. He is in the robin's tummy.

**Mummy:**
I am sure that Jesus can find the poor caterpillar.
Death itself is a treasure box, it doesn't matter how did you die and where your body is laid. We all shall be in the treasure box of death itself because we are all treasures of God. Where we are, where the treasure box is. We define the treasure box, not the other way around.

**Arabella:**
The snail carries his treasure box at all time
He lives in his shell and he dies in his shell.
He shall be resurrected in his shell.

**Mummy:**
Wow, that's a beautiful poem Arabella!
I am so proud of you

**Arabella:**
Do you think the snail can still remember me when he is resurrected from his death?

**Mummy:**
Will you remember your old mummy when you are resurrected from your death?

**Arabella:**
Of course mummy.
I will remember you forever and ever.

**Mummy:**
Well, in case your memory fade,
You can upload me onto a computer
And make sure that the internet is fast,
So it won't be just loading and loading when you searching for me...

*Mummy and Arabella laugh together.*

**Arabella:**
Where are we going to be living after we are resurrected when Jesus comes again?
**Mummy:**
Could be anywhere in the universe.
Planet earth, Mars, Moon, or we could go to other universes within our multi-universe like Alice's rabbit hole, or we could live in different places at one time like Jesus lives in our hearts and lives in heaven.
**Arabella:**
How many universes are in the multi-universes mummy? Would I have to become very small like Alice to get through the gate to the beautiful garden? Am I going to be invisible like Jesus or visible with a beautiful dress?
**Mummy:**
I don't know my dear, what do you think and want?
**Arabella:**
Well, I think I shall have tea parties on the earth, Moon and Mars at the same time with my most beautiful pink dress with flowers. And I want to be invisible when I play hide and seek with my friends, no one will see me when I hide and I'll become visible again to scare them all.
I think I want to be in a space rocket with big fire tail when I visit multiple universes, it is more exciting than go through a rabbit hole.
**Mummy:**
well, you won't be needing a space rocket anymore when you are resurrected after death. You will be free to travel to whenever you want.

## Easter Sunday, 12th of April 2020

**Arabella:**
With wings like the angles?
**Mummy:**
With the wings of your thought, perhaps more effective.
**Arabella:**
I am thinking I am on Mars now.
**Mummy:**
I am thinking I am on the earth and on Mars at the same time now. Can you see me on earth from Mars Arabella?
**Arabella:**
Yes, mummy, I can see you! But you look very tiny on earth!!
**Mummy:**
Well, you are even smaller than me.
I will need to get my telescope out to look at you on Mars now.
**Arabella:**
Hurray, let's look at Mars with our telescope.

Mummy takes out the telescope and they observe space.

**Arabella:**
Will there be Coronavirus on Mars?
**Mummy:**
Not sure, what do you think?
**Arabella:**
I don't know, maybe we can live forever on Mars if there is no Coronavirus.
**Mummy:**
The Coronavirus won't be able to kill those people that can live forever or those people being resurrected from death.
**Arabella:**
What is the difference?
**Mummy:**
Difference of what?
**Arabella:**
Difference between living forever and resurrection after death.
**Mummy:**
We will have to find out by ourselves.

**Arabella:**
How about you find out what is living forever and I find out what is being resurrected after death.

**Mummy:**
Why?

**Arabella:**
I'd like to die and hide in a treasure box and Jesus treasure hunt me. It is more fun that way!

**Mummy:**
Well then, I will need to figure out what I am going to do and going to do and going to do. . ..for my never ending life.

**Arabella:**
Are you going to be bored without me?

**Mummy:**
I would have to hope that Jesus finds you sooner than later.

*Mummy and Arabella laugh together.*

# 9 days after Ascension Day, 30th of May 2020

*Arabella and Mummy are under the cherry tree in the evening.*

**Mummy:**
Arabella, SpaceX is sending the astronauts Robert and Douglas into orbit in Florida now.
Shall we have a look through our telescope, perhaps we can see them ascending into the heavens.
**Arabella:**
Like Jesus ascending into heaven on Ascension Day?
**Mummy:**
Well, the astronauts are going to the space filled with stars we call the heavens, it is within our space and can be reached within time. The heaven where Jesus went is a space beyond the limit of our space and time. And Jesus did not need a space rocket to go and he will be back most likely without a space rocket. The astronauts need a space rocket to go and a space rocket to return, well, at least for now.
And we don't know the exact location of Jesus in heaven and we don't know when he will return.
But we know exactly where the astronauts are in the heavens, they are going to be at the International Space Station, where is 262 miles above the earth and the space rocket is controlled from SpaceX Kennedy centre in Florida. It takes 19 hours for the space rocket to reach the ISS and they will stay there for a few months before they return to earth.

**Arabella:**
Why we don't know when Jesus will come back? Is it a secret?
**Mummy:**
It is a secret because we do not know but it is not a secret to the people who know.
**Arabella:**
Who knows when Jesus will be back? Can they tell me the secret—I am very good at keeping secrets.
**Mummy:**
I don't know who knows the date of Jesus's return. I would have already told you who to ask if I knew, I am terrible at keeping secret as you know.
**Arabella:**
Yes, you are terrible at keeping secrets mummy. You always tell me what is my surprise present.
**Mummy:**
Hehe, let's see whether we can see the astronauts in their space rocket through our telescope, shall we?
**Arabella:**
We might see both Jesus and the astronauts.
**Mummy:**
That would be marvellous my dear!

*They look towards the sky under the cherry tree through telescope.*

**Arabella:**
Mummy, if we go to Mars before we die, and Jesus comes back to the earth, we would have missed him.
**Mummy:**
Good point Arabella. Shall we wait for Jesus on the planet earth then.
**Arabella:**
I want to go to Mars too. . . . .how about we leave Jesus a letter on earth before we go to Mars, he will come to Mars to find us, like leaving him a map for treasure hunt you know.

## 9 DAYS AFTER ASCENSION DAY, 30TH OF MAY 2020

**Mummy:**
Oh, very thoughtful of you Arabella.
But I am not sure that Jesus needs the map, but let's do it anyway.
**Arabella:**
And I shall draw him a beautiful map as I am good at drawing, you can write him a beautiful poem as a riddle because you are a writer. That would make the treasure hunt much more fun for him.
**Mummy:**
That's very thoughtful Arabella.
How about those people who can not draw like you and write like mummy? Wouldn't it be helpful if we could provide Jesus a treasure hunt map to find everyone on Mars and on the earth.
**Arabella:**
That's a great idea mummy.
We surely should put everyone who died from the Coronavirus on our treasure hunt map for Jesus.
**Mummy:**
How about the black man called George Floyd I told you about who was killed this Monday by police?
**Arabella:**
Of course, I can draw the city he was killed in America on earth.
Why did the police kill him Mummy?
**Mummy:**
I don't know Arabella, people have been killing each other for a long time now, one reason or another.
**Arabella:**
We don't kill people or animals. We are vegans.
**Mummy:**
Yes, Arabella, good girl.
Look at the beautiful drawings and paintings you have produced, they are beautiful and reminds me of the Divine. You see, we humans are capable of creating the beauty of divine through arts, music, sending space rockets to the moon and to Mars and one day we might be able to create Artificial Intelligence capable of doing everything like us, but we also fight for toilet paper, steal other people's bread and kill the people we dislike because of skin colour.

**Arabella:**
Why do we humans kill each other mummy?
**Mummy:**
Because we are not the snail who does not need to wait for the Messiah.
We have been waiting for the Messiah to save us from the blood of our brothers for thousands of years.
**Arabella:**
How do you know the snail does not need to wait for the Messiah Mummy?
**Mummy:**
Because I have a mind to think even though I do not always think right. The snail might also need, who knows.
**Arabella:**
When Jesus comes again, would he help us to change into better persons?
**Mummy:**
Well, we would have to try our best to transform ourselves while we are waiting, otherwise we will become the snail.
**Arabella:**
What's wrong with being the snail?
**Mummy:**
Nothing wrong, just a bit. . ..bored. . ..
**Arabella:**
You think the snail is bored mummy?
**Mummy:**
I think he is bored, but not necessarily He is bored.
**Arabella:**
Let's ask him.
Snail, are you bored?
**Snail:**
Silence.
**Arabella:**
Snail, are you bored?
**Snail:**
Silence.

## 9 DAYS AFTER ASCENSION DAY, 30TH OF MAY 2020

**Arabella:**
Mummy, the snail does not answer me?
**Mummy:**
I know. He never does.
**Arabella:**
You said you have heard him talking before.
**Mummy:**
Yes, I said that but he didn't necessarily.
**Arabella:**
Oh, bother.
**Mummy:**
The cherries all fallen now. We will have to wait to see the cherry blossom next Easter.
**Mummy:**
Will be Coronavirus be gone next Spring? Can I have a play date with Alexander next Easter? I want to hunt for Easter eggs.
**Mummy:**
Hopefully the virus has stopped and you can have a play date with your friends and we can hunt for Easter eggs in the pine forest of Tallinn, Estonia.
**Arabella:**
Hooray, I love the pine forest.
Will Jesus return next Easter mummy?
**Mummy:**
May be.
**Arabella:**
If he doesn't.
We can always wait for him next Easter.
**Mummy:**
There is no such thing as next Easter Arabella.
All we have is this Easter.
**Arabella:**
Are you sad mummy?
**Mummy:**
A little. The Spring has just ended. The lock down has just loosened. You are going back to school this Monday.

**Arabella:**
I can't wait to go back to school Mummy.
**Mummy:**
I am not very sad actually.
I had you during the lock down.
Many people were on their own, alone with the alone.
Thank you Arabella for being with me all this time this Easter.
**Arabella:**
Mummy, do you want a little cuddle?
**Mummy:**
of course, a cuddle always good.

*Mummy and Arabella cuddle with each other under the cherry tree.*

**Mummy:**
Arabella, lets sing the Lord's prayer together, shall we?
**Arabella:**
I sing first, I sing first.
**Mummy:**
You sing first my dear, I shall accompany you with my harp.

**Arabella:**
Our father which art in heaven,
Hallowed be thy name
Thy kingdom come
Thy will be done
On earth as it is in heaven
Give us this day our daily bread
Forgive our trespasses
As we forgive those who trespass against us
Lead us not into temptation
But deliver us from evil
For thy is the kingdom, the power and the glory are your
Now and forever
Amen.

### 9 DAYS AFTER ASCENSION DAY, 30TH OF MAY 2020

*Arabella and Mummy start to paint the face of George Floyd, and many faces of the dead from Coronavirus appear on the big screen while they are painting. They sing the Lord's Prayer together.*

*Mummy and Arabella sing the Lord's Prayer in Aramaic together:*
Abunde-vashmaia
Negtadash-shishmaja
Titl-malcuta newe-sevianak
Aykana-devashaia adbahara
Alan-lagma desunkana niaumana
Bash-bucalan jauvai
Aykana dafegnan eshvagna lejaivain
Ulta-talan lemesiuna
Elataxan membish
Amin
...Amen

*Light goes gradually, in a deem of light, a poem being read accompanied by harp:*

**Divine But Not Mine**
Is a drop of water of the ocean ocean?
If not
What is ocean?

Is a tiny daisy flower in the spring field spring?
If not
What is spring?

Is this beautiful moment of time time?
If not
What is time?

Is my love within this tiny heart love?
If not

What is love?

Am I, an image of Divine Divine?
If not
What is Divine?

A drop of water of the ocean has never called himself ocean
A daisy of the spring field has never called herself spring
But why
The beauty of a beautiful moment
So fractional
And shine light in the infinity of time
But why
My love within this tiny heart
So small
And bring love to love all measure forgotten
I, an image of divine
So broken
But broken just like the divine
I gently call
Rise again
This drop of water of the ocean
I gently call
Rise again
That daisy of the spring field
But I could not call the beautiful moment of time
To rise again
I could not call the love within my tiny heart
To rise again
I could not call an image of divine
To rise again

I sail in the ocean of water drops
I walk in the spring field of daisies

*9 days after Ascension Day, 30th of May 2020*

I Enjoy the beautiful moments of time in time
With love in this tiny heart
Divine but not mine.

The End.

# Drawings

The following drawings were created by Arabella Elizabeth Stell during the Easter season 2020, who is the daughter of Rainbow Chang the author of this book. Arabella just turned 4 years old at that time. Arabella is a finalist of UK & International Emerging Artist Award 2020, VAO.

www.ingramcontent.com/pod-product-compliance
Lightning Source LLC
Chambersburg PA
CBHW070517090426
42735CB00012B/2819